First Facts®

Earn It, Save It, Spend It!

Earn Money

by Emily Raij

raintree
a Capstone company — publishers for children

Raintree is an imprint of Capstone Global Library Limited, a company incorporated in England and Wales having its registered office at 264 Banbury Road, Oxford, OX2 7DY – Registered company number: 6695582

www.raintree.co.uk
myorders@raintree.co.uk

Edited by Karen Aleo
Designed by Sarah Bennett
Picture research by Tracy Cummins
Production by Kathy McColley
Originated by Capstone Global Library Ltd
Printed and bound in India

ISBN 978 1 4747 8156 5 (hardback)
ISBN 978 1 4747 8160 2 (paperback)

British Library Cataloguing in Publication Data
A full catalogue record for this book is available from the British Library.

Acknowledgements
Capstone Studio: Karon Dubke, Design Element; iStockphoto: ljubaphoto, 13; Shutterstock: Adam Gilchrist, Back Cover, ANURAK PONGPATIMET, 21, baibaz, 5, DedMityay, 9, Dragon Images, 15, Maria Evseyeva, 17, Monkey Business Images, 11, Nik Merkulov, Design Element, olavs, Cover, oliveromg, 19, Roman Samborskyi, 7

Contents

CHAPTER 1

Why do people earn money?

People use money to pay for the things they need and the things they want. Needs are things such as food, housing and clothing. Not everything that people buy is a need. Sometimes people buy things they would like to have.

To have this money, most people have to earn it. They work and get paid for doing the work.

When people earn money for work, they receive money, or pay. They have to make decisions about what to do with their pay. People can spend, save or **donate** money. It's important for people to make good decisions with their money. First they must pay for things they need.

FACT
Once money is spent, that money is not available any more. More money for things will then have to be earned.

donate to give something as a gift to a charity or cause

If people have money left after paying for the things they need, they can put it in a savings account at the bank. By saving a little money each week or month, they can get enough to pay for something big, such as a car or a holiday.

Loans

Sometimes people do not have the money to make a big purchase. If they cannot save the money, banks can provide **loans**. Loans are money given to someone to make a purchase. Loans are paid back to the bank by the person who borrowed the money.

deposit to put money into a bank account

withdraw to take money out of a bank account

loan money that is borrowed with a plan to pay it back

budget a plan for spending money

They can **deposit** money into the bank account and **withdraw** money when they need it.

Many people create a plan for saving and spending money. This is called a **budget**. A budget shows how much money can be earned, spent and saved.

CHAPTER 2

Ways to earn money

How do people earn money for the things they need and want? They have a job! There are many types of jobs. Some people sell **goods** in shops. Some of the money made by selling the goods pays the people who work in the shop.

FACT
Companies make money by selling goods for more than they cost to make. This money is called **profit**.

goods things that can be bought or sold

profit the money that a business makes after expenses have been paid

Other people provide **services**. A service is work that helps others. Teachers, doctors and car mechanics provide services. They get paid for the service.

On the job

Different skills and knowledge are needed for different jobs. Some people go to college to learn these skills. Others receive training at their job. Doctors go to university. Then they complete their training in a hospital.

service work that helps others, such as providing medical care, fixing cars or cutting hair

Some people start their own businesses. They make and sell goods or provide services.

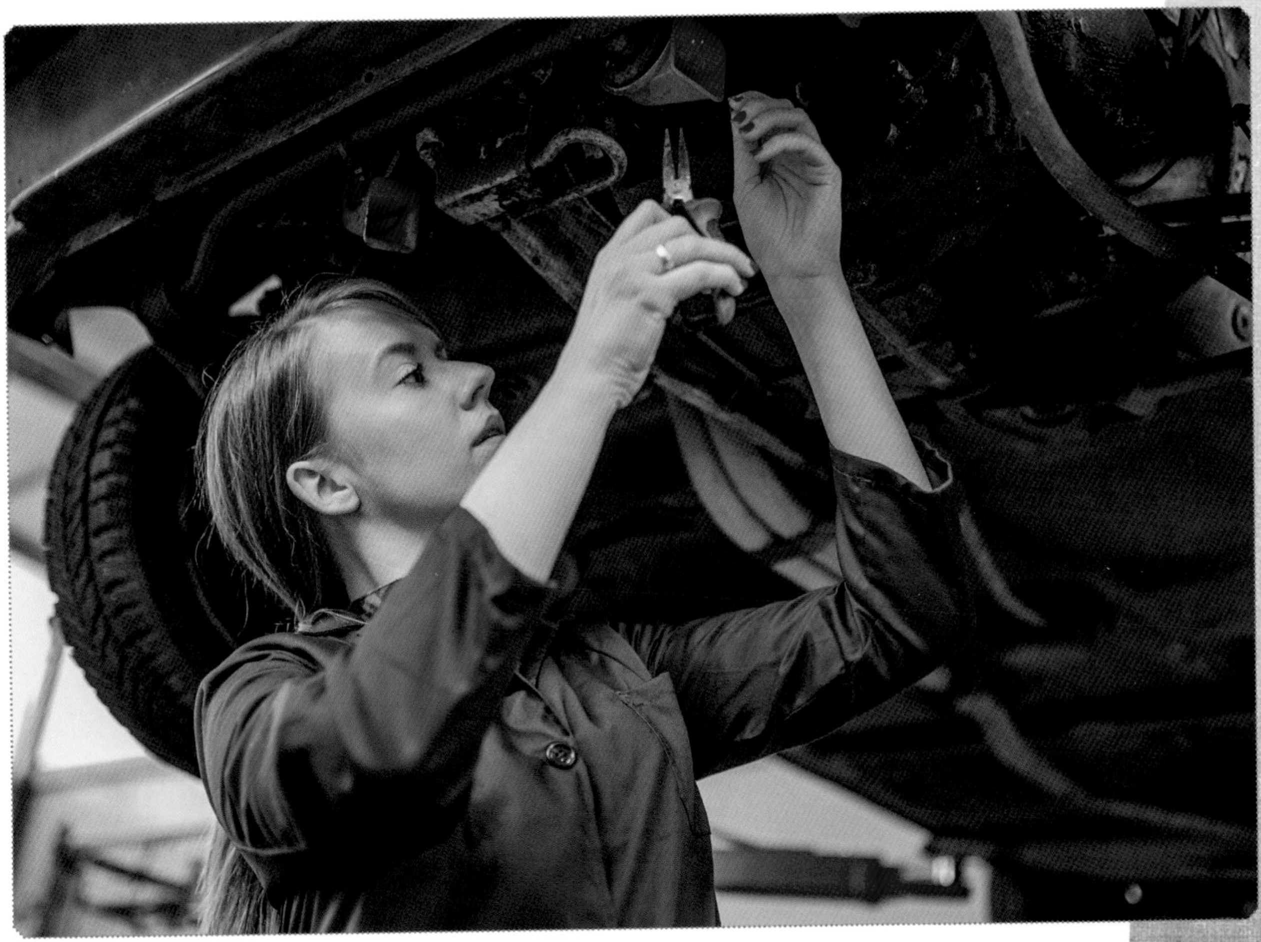

Companies and organizations pay **employees**. Many companies put this payment straight into the employees' bank accounts. Employees can use this money at any time. Some workers are paid with a paper cheque. They deposit this into their bank account. Then they can take the money out and spend it. Employees can also be paid in cash. These notes and coins are the **currency** people use to buy things.

employee someone who works for a company and is paid by the company

organization people joined together for a certain purpose

currency the type of money a country uses

CHAPTER 3

Try it!

Think of a service you can provide. There are lots of ways you can earn money in your neighbourhood. And you'll be helping your neighbours at the same time! Ask neighbours if they need help with jobs around their houses or gardens. Lots of little jobs can turn into steady **income**.

FACT

Neighbours often need help walking their dogs, raking leaves or washing their cars.

income money that you get

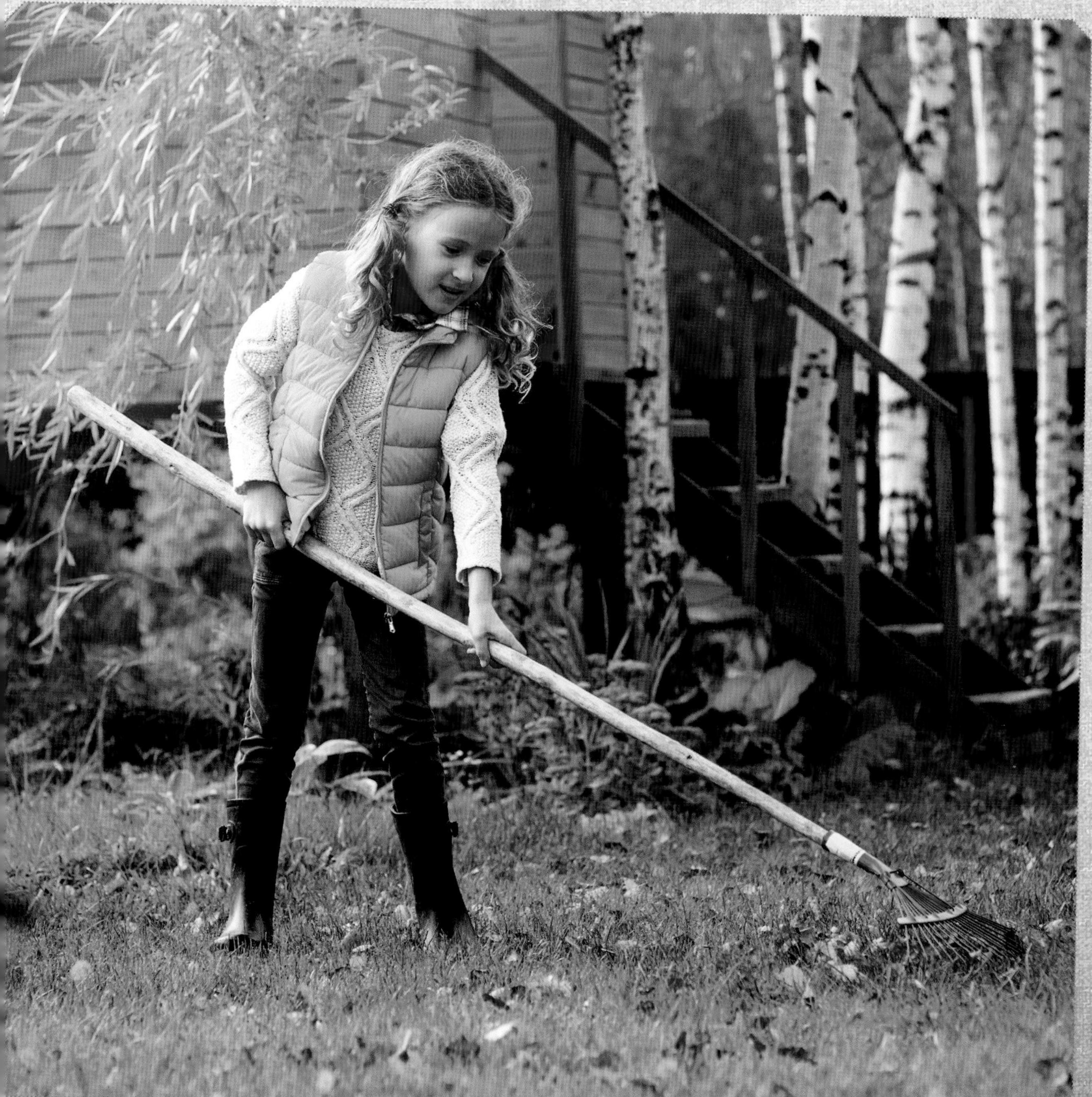

Selling goods is another way to make money. You can make crafts, such as jewellery or artwork. With an adult's help, have a garden sale or go to a car boot sale to sell these crafts. You can sell things you no longer use too. If you have a garden sale, put up signs with the date, time and place of your sale.

What are the reasons you want to earn money? Make a list of goals, such as buying a new computer game. Then work out how long it will take to earn the money. As you earn money, save it until you have enough to meet your goal. You need to save to have money to spend!

Glossary

budget a plan for spending money

currency the type of money a country uses

deposit to put money into a bank account

donate to give something as a gift to a charity or cause

employee someone who works for a company and is paid by the company

goods things that can be bought or sold

income money that you get

loan money that is borrowed with a plan to pay it back

profit the money that a business makes after expenses have been paid

service work that helps others, such as providing medical care, fixing cars or cutting hair

withdraw to take money out of a bank account

Find out more

Managing Your Money, Jane Bingham and Holly Bathie (Usborne, 2019)

The Kids' Money Book: Earning, Saving Spending, Investing, Donating (Jamie Kyle McGillian (Sterling, 2016)

Build Your Business series, Tammy Gagne (Raintree, 2018)

Websites and apps

Try the Rooster Money app. It helps you keep track of your pocket money and your spending. You can also set goals for saving.

These websites have fun games and videos to help you understand money and make good spending choices:

www.bbc.com/bitesize/topics/zp8dmp3
www.bbc.com/bitesize/topics/z8yv4wx

Comprehension questions

1. What are some ways people earn money? How can you earn money?
2. What are some reasons people earn money?
3. Should people spend all their money straight away? Why or why not?

Index